The
Unconquerables

SALUTES TO THE UNDYING
SPIRIT OF THE NAZI-OCCUPIED COUNTRIES

BY

JOSEPH AUSLANDER

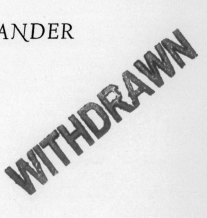

SIMON AND SCHUSTER

NEW YORK, 1943

ABOUT THE APPEARANCE OF BOOKS IN WARTIME

A recent ruling by the War Production Board has curtailed the use of paper by book publishers in 1943.

In line with this ruling and in order to conserve materials and manpower, we are co-operating by:

1. Using lighter-weight paper, which reduces the bulk of our books substantially.
2. Printing books with smaller margins and with more words to each page. Result: fewer pages per book.

Slimmer and smaller books will save paper and plate metal and labor. We are sure that readers will understand the publishers' desire to co-operate as fully as possible with the objectives of the War Production Board and our government.

MANUFACTURED IN THE UNITED STATES OF AMERICA
BY HADDON CRAFTSMEN, SCRANTON, PENNSYLVANIA

For
Stephen Vincent Benét

Dear Steve,
Because, by your gallant life and death and by
your brave words at work, you set for our time the
noblest example of the poet in action, I beg you
to brood like a gentle spirit over these lines, nor
turn away your face from

Your Friend,
Joe

ACKNOWLEDGMENT

For permission to reprint certain of the poems in this book I thank the editors of *The Saturday Evening Post, This Week, The New York Times,* and *The Washington Post.*

CONTENTS

DEDICATION: TO THE UNCONQUERABLES   3

APPEAL TO OUR POETS   4

LETTER TO THE UNCONQUERABLE FRENCH   5

NOVEMBER ELEVENTH   9

LETTER TO THE UNCONQUERABLE CZECHOSLOVAKS   11

ZERO-HOUR MEDITATION   14

LETTER TO THE UNCONQUERABLE NORWEGIANS   15

POSTSCRIPT FROM FINLAND   21

LETTER TO THE UNCONQUERABLE POLES   23

LETTER TO AN ENGLISH FRIEND   29

LETTER TO THE UNCONQUERABLE DUTCH   30

THE RISING TIDE   36

LETTER TO THE UNCONQUERABLE BELGIANS   38

THESE EVENINGS   45

LETTER TO THE UNCONQUERABLE GREEKS   46

ELEGY IN AUTUMN   50

LETTER TO THE UNCONQUERABLE LUXEMBOURGERS   51

TARGET FOR TONIGHT   53

LETTER TO THE UNCONQUERABLE YUGOSLAVS   54

DUNKERQUE ANNIVERSARY   58

DEDICATION: TO THE UNCONQUERABLES

All that is here, said and unsaid,
All that I tried to say—still try—
I dedicate to you, the dead,
To you who are about to die.

To you, uprooted from your place,
The starving tortured multitude,
Although I cannot see your face,
I know your heart beats unsubdued.

I know, I feel the stubborn flame,
Your hunger and your hope I feel,
O heroes whom I cannot name,
Upon whose necks Hate grinds his heel.

I know your wounds, your blood I know,
Your agony and death are mine;
I clench my fists, I bear the blow,
Their bullets also split my spine.

I love you and I take your hand,
Your broken bones and dreams I take,
And darkly you will understand
These words I set down for your sake.

APPEAL TO OUR POETS

Heavy upon the heart the world's great wrong
Grinds night and day a grim goose-stepping boot;
We set our mouths for singing, but the song
Sickens against the tongue like Dead Sea fruit.

We have no harp, we have no willow tree,
Lord of our unconsumed and quenchless dust;
The anguish of the people's misery
Finds neither voice nor wisdom it can trust.

Where are the poets, keepers of our glory,
Kindlers of faith and courage, what of them?
Where are the prophets who can tell our story,
That we may not forget Jerusalem?

O poets, rise and sing, however hard
The words may come, however minds may grope
For the true breath and passion of the bard,
For the true trumpet of our living hope!

Sing, though the soul be sick and disbelieve
The song, until the singer's furious art
Arouse the spirit lest too long it grieve,
Awake the heavy and oblivious heart!

4

LETTER TO THE UNCONQUERABLE FRENCH

O Jehanne, with the trumpets in your name
By all the lilies of the oriflamme,
By all the faggots and the final shame,
By all the burning voices at the tree,
By all the visions that we cannot see,
By all you were that we can never be,
By all the little lambs, by every lark
That spilled a fiery fountain, spark on spark,
Of music to your heart, Jehanne of Arc,
By all your simple strength, and by the few
Straight words like light, and by the dream that grew
In your gray well-spaced eyes until you knew
The work you had to do—
The glory that flared up, and darkened, and withdrew,
The death they did to you—

Is this your France that made the great horn blow
Across the blood-red gap at Roncevaux?
Are these the mighty men
Who time and time again
Rebuffed the Roman, broke the Saracen?
Is this indeed the Gaul
Who stood, a terrible and living wall
Of flesh and blood and bone and spirit's pith compounded,
Forged in the furnaces of hell,
A solid mass

Chanting with hoarse monotonous iteration
The battle cry of a beleaguered nation,
"They shall not pass!"
(Christ, how that cry resounded!)
And drove the guttural and gloating Hun
Back from the very citadel
Of desperate Verdun,
Depleted and defeated and confounded?

Oh, flash again, bright shield and furious lance,
And save the soul of France!
Strike down the traitor, cut the coward down,
The wolf and buzzard running beak to fang
In field and town.
Ring out, as yesterday you rang,
Clarion of hope, bugle of liberation,
To a bewildered and heroic nation
By knave and lout
Sold out,
The furtive coin clenched in the shameless fist
Of dupe and parricide and terrorist!

Ah, France, beloved, brave and beautiful land,
On every side they stand,
On every hand
The dear magnificent dead,
A glorious ghostly band—
Roland and Oliver and Charlemagne,

And the tall Paladins who fought and bled
And with the uncounted slain
Fattened the kites of Spain;
And that bright-bearded captain-king whose name
Is a shooting star,
A flying flame—
Navarre!

And she,
The gallant martyr maid of Domremy,
Who, when the hearts of men grew faint,
Rallied for Dauphin and for Saint Denis,
Soldier and saint,
The swords that set France free!
Ah sweet Jehanne, Jehanne,
Now that the spirits of your people languish,
And the grim traps are laid,
The sordid ambuscade
Wherein, convulsed with unendurable anguish,
France is once more betrayed;
Ah, let your piercing clarion
Shatter this hideous trance,
This nightmare sickness in the soul of France!
Refuse this foul infection,
And, by the virtue of that proud rejection,
Rekindle, repossess
The sacred fire, the ancient fearlessness!

France is one vast Bastille;
The people turning and twisting under a vicious heel:
Your France, whose blood-soaked pikestaff banners gave
New hope to the oppressed, the prisoner, the slave;
Your France, that raised the heart like Lazarus from the grave,
Bends now her neck in the vile dust to kiss
A monstrous parody of peace.

Ride on, Jehanne, ride on and on and on
Through the thick darkness ringing your clarion!
Lightning of long deliverance,
Jehanne of France,
Jehanne! Jehanne! Jehanne!

NOVEMBER ELEVENTH

I gaze at autumn and the slow gold weather,
And yet I know this is no honeyed peace:
The shadow running under the flying feather,
The grass fear-furrowed with the lightning's crease
Too clearly indicate a treacherous tether.

As to behold the hawk, that black sky-rider,
Swoop to the kill, a murderous marauder;
Or watch upon his burning wheel, no wider
Than death's bright breathless anxious inch, no broader,
That prince of polished treachery, the spider:

Is but to recognize in this their hour
Of easy triumph mid the world's morass
The foul familiar pattern of such power
As lurks in pitfalls of the sunny grass,
The ambush-cloud, the trap behind the bower.

This is the time of death and brave decay;
The languid obsequies of summer done,
The lime trees yellow on Champs Élysées,
The lovely shell, the shining skeleton
Tuned to a treacherous November day.

9

This is the time when we remember most
The great hope of that morning buried alive:
The lime trees blazoned forth the golden Host,
Eyes burned to see Millennium arrive,
Hearts hushed the footfall of the Holy Ghost. . . .

And now all's horror—bullet, ax, and rope—
Those posthumous implacable eyes accuse
The generations that betrayed their hope,
The greed and blindness that betrayed their truce,
The peace that perished ere its roots could grope.

Lo, one more feverish tragic autumn dying
In a great blaze like some forgotten king
Whose warriors range about his body crying,
Though to their heavy hearts the shrill fifes ring:
"Yet, Freedom, yet thy banner, torn but flying! . . ."

LETTER TO THE UNCONQUERABLE CZECHOSLOVAKS

This is not a letter that starts,
"Dear So-and-So,"
And ends,
"Faithfully yours." Ah no,
Brave hearts
And gallant friends,
This is a letter that a man,
Heavy with words, makes;
In my case, an ordinary American,
Whose hand shakes
Because, knowing the tremendous truth,
The words choke up in his mouth.

My mind goes back to Munich,
Goes back to the beginning—
The little Caesar, hand upraised, hand in tunic,
Gaping and glaring and grinning
Under his mustache; the cheers,
The "Sieg Heils" dinning
Drunken music in his ears;
My mind goes back
To the cowardly bivouac
Under the umbrella, under
The alpine parasol where you were torn asunder
To appease the Nazi appetite for plunder.

You were the blood-bright spur
To prick the languid conscience of this age;
You were the cage
Wherein the Executioner
(That archsadist,
Of all mad dogs the maddest)
Might practice the refinements of his rage;
The laboratory, soundproof, leisurely, clinical,
Where, quite begloved, bespatted, monocled and cynical,
The Fiend could vent
In hideous experiment
His hate of God and man, of saint and sage.

Hangmen die too:
Bullets from nowhere through the spine
Make hangmen whine,
Turn hangmen's faces blue;
If they have long enough to remember,
They may recall
The name of one Jan Opletal,
Young medical student at Prague:
His death from wounds in the night,
His funeral. . . .
The seventeenth of November:
The streets churning with Czech youth; the sudden brawl
Deliberately provoked; the foremost fall,
Shot down by storm troopers; they lurch, they sprawl;
A few crawl

Away to die like any beaten dog:
This is only the curtain raiser; the epilogue
Follows: the student hostels are surrounded;
Boys and girls riddled by *Schmeissers*, tortured, abused,
            pounded
Into submission; eyes gouged out, ear lobes torn off, hounded
From horror to horror. . . . Turn your face to the wall,
Hangman: death will soon enfold in fog
The sickening sound, the smell, the sight
Of this blood-soaked Walpurgis Night.

But never, hangman, never from your face
Shall death or time or blood erase
That massacre of youth,
Nor any self-dug death pits hide one trace
Of their fierce love of truth;
Break the head
Of every stubborn hostage; shoot him dead
Until the earth runs red—
Others will stand in his stead;
You sow the dragon's tooth:
Burn a hundred Lidices to the ground:
New Lidices will spring up: the desolate space
Charred, choked with ashes,
And dead birds all around,
Will consecrate a holy place
Drenched with the blood that flames and flashes
Wherever Czechoslovaks and freedom's dream are found.

ZERO-HOUR MEDITATION

Now that the days of peace depart,
Now that the locusts scourge the land,
The bullet rushing to my heart
Is hurled, or halted, by Thy hand.

To none of all Thy creatures, none,
Thy patience and compassion move
As to this little willful one
Thou dost so curiously love.

This is the hour myself may see
(Where men are cruel, muddled, blind)
Thy fierce inflexibility
Cold as their hearts, but far more kind.

LETTER TO THE UNCONQUERABLE NORWEGIANS

I know you, Norway;
Your blood runs bright in my little daughter,
Your beauty runs warm and wild
In my girl child:
You are a queen, standing in a doorway,
Staring out over the long water,
Remembering the ships
(Remembering the boys and girls with yellow hair
And the laughter struck dead on their lips).
You are a woman with a beautiful name,
Remembering how the new barbarians came,
The red night sky and the slaughter,
The treachery and the shame
(And when it was all finished, the smell of death in the air,
The shambles and the flame).

I remember you, Norway; I shall always remember
Your good hills, thickets, groves, and your great mountains
Phosphorescent with snow against the brilliant umber
Of clouds billowing like fountains
In a fire-brushed blue sky;
I shall remember until I die
Your waterfalls everywhere,
Waterfalls that dive down a turbulent stair
Into chasms boiling a livid rose,
Waterfalls with the rain's and the sun's bows

Burning together on their hearts like blood-red brooches—
(These things the mind knows;
These things the memory approaches)—
And the dark glens and the forests of fir
Whose steep black streamers
Twinkle green on the wind-rocked light—
(Ah, the light blowing, the flakes of light blowing,
As if the sun were snowing!)—
And keep all dreamers
Awake in the summer night
When the whole atmosphere
Is soaked through with the dust of stars and pine
Powdered fine:
And trees, liquid and luminous, and here and there
(Clumps of the orange-berried ash, families of birches)
Moving among them the apple-colored cows
Nudge the wet night and breathe and browse,
And the bird-crowded hedges,
And the dawn's dew-washed edges
Glitter—
And the dawn thrills and thickens with the birds' twitter.

I see you as I saw you long ago,
Standing so,
Lingering in the doorway
Of your blue water,
O noble Norway
(Whose blood runs bright in my little daughter).

The evening was warm,
The twilight long,
The summer sun
Fastened gold fingernails to the horizon in a slow
Reluctant afterglow.
(That was before the storm,
That was before the blow,
That was before the Hun,
The steel-winged swarm
Swept the sweet land with flame.
That was before the new barbarians came.)

I remember the small farms,
And the hard soil,
And the heavy toil
That covers the countryside
With harvests of courage and pride,
And the women with open arms
Welcoming the sickly German lad
(That was after the last war,
Long before this horror, Oh long before!);
Giving the German boys the best they had,
Feeding them at the table with their own sons—
These were the same, the very same
Who came back later, who came
With slaughter and flame,
With tanks and guns,
With bayonets and bombs

To the friendly homes,
To their foster fathers and mothers,
To their foster sisters and brothers,
Speaking the language with all its charms,
Spouting all its graces,
Spitting it into the people's faces.

What is there left to tell?
How shall I start?
Proud land I love so well,
Proud people so close to my heart?
I see you as I saw you that last long summer
(Before the bomber
Let loose hell,
Before the sky fell
In flame).
You are the same proud people, yet not the same:
Your eyes are frozen blue steel,
Your mouths are stone,
Your hands hard as bone;
There are faces I do not see, but feel.
Many are gone:
Some dead, never mind how, just dead
For something their hands did, their mouths said,
Their eyes read;
Some fled
In little fishing boats, in leaky crates,
By night, on skis, on skates,

To England, to Canada, to the United States;
Some stained the snow, the water, the ground;
Some drowned
And were never found.

And what ghosts looked on!—
Harald the Fairhair, Olav Tryggvasson,
Olav the Saint
(You must not fail them, must not falter, must not faint!),
Peter Tordenskjold
(Hold on! Hold on! Hold!),
Wergeland, Welhaven, Sverdrup
(Eyes straight ahead! Chins up!),
Björnson, Ibsen, Nansen . . . and ah, the new martyrs at gaze,
The patriots of the Sixty Immortal Days!

They will return,
O Norway, mother of heroes,
Mother of patriots,
Mother of men!
They will come back from everywhere—
By ocean, land, and air—
They will come back, and then. . . .
There will be shots;
They will burn
The filth of the Nazi Neros:
There will be a tremendous house-cleaning.
The sky will be washed free

Of the foulness, the infamy.
Your young eagles will give the sky over Norway a new
      meaning.
Every street, house, factory,
Every farm and field
Will have to be cauterized and healed:
This will take time, beloved land,
But I shall again see you stand
Like a queen called home from heroic exile, the church bells
      ringing,
The people crying and laughing and shouting and singing! . . .
You will look out over the long blue water,
The clean light on your hair
As you linger there
In your doorway
(Ah, dear mother of my little daughter!),
Norway!

POSTSCRIPT FROM FINLAND

In the frozen forests of Finland
They say the soldiers sleep
Where the snows of Tolvajarvi
Cover them deep.

An arm sticks up like cordwood,
A leg juts out bent double,
A face thrusts sharp, unshaven
With stiff black stubble.

This is the forest of sleepers,
The forest of flat white faces,
The forest of boots and helmets
And broken traces.

This is the forest of glory
For the seven sons of Ivan:
Sleep, you lads like statues,
Rest if you can.

Forget the girls in the homeland
Whose letters stiffened with you:
They will stop writing letters
And forget too.

21

Only the snows of the forest
And the moon with her frozen light
And the stars that go staring forever
Down the deep night—

Only these will not forget you
Till the brief and most brilliant spring
When from your skulls on a sudden
Something will sing;

Even your eyeballs will bustle
With tiny inquisitive roots;
Maybe a harebell will marry
One of your boots;

Maybe your long locks will furnish
Moss for the marten's nest—
Sleep, it is best to say nothing:
Silence is best.

LETTER TO THE UNCONQUERABLE POLES

O martyred Poland, brave and tragic Poles,
O people with stout hearts and stalwart souls,
People of poetry, music, cathedrals, colleges, courage, and
      beauty,
People with a proud imperative sense of honor and duty,
People with a long and noble history,
People of sorrow and mystery,
People of so many a dark hour, in this your darkest hour,
When, by the Hunnish lust for blood and power,
The flower
Of Polish manhood lies despoiled and spent
And spilt
In flame and ruin; all your strength had built,
The glowing monument,
The glory of your spirit and your mind
Abused and rifled, hammered black and blind;
The altars of your faith defiled,
And with lewd rites reviled,
And broken
(Poor twisted shells where late the Lord had spoken!)
Under the savage chariots of lust
In the indifferent dust
For any passing dog to find!

You were the first
Who, with unbandaged eyes,

Faced his abominable lies,
His foul obscenities,
And branded him accurst;
Confronted the full fury of the foe
And calmly answered "No!"
Of all the others, none
Had dared this thing, had done
What you, knowing the worst,
So proudly and so resolutely durst.
Against your granite valor burst
The monstrous tides of agony, wave on wave,
That blotted out the sun
And left your land a grave.

You alone
Had always known
During a thousand years,
In torture and in tears,
How little one could trust
The Teuton in his lust;
You clearly saw
What all the others had refused to see:
The hideous futility
Of faith in Nazi covenant or law
Or oath, however solemn it might be,
Sealed howsoever with solemnity,
When sworn to by that swine of treachery;
You set it in the light

Of Poland burning bright,
Of Warsaw blazing day and night,
Of thousands upon thousands dying left and right,
That here was one
Whose only law was perfidy
And blood and appetite!

After one thousand years of "only"—
The immemorial German word,
The immemorial German way—
They want "only" Danzig today,
That is to say,
Much to their heartfelt sorrow,
They want "only" Pomerania tomorrow,
"Only" Gdynia, "only" Bogumin, "only" one third
Of this or that rich wheat land, languishing and lonely
Of course to feel the tramp of the Teutonic herd. . . .
Nothing absurd,
It is an old song,
And the list of "onlys" is long:
From Geron to Hitler the carrion birds of prey
Croak "only, only, only," tearing away
Land and faith from the Poles, but the Poles stay.

After nineteen days of hell,
Warsaw fell.
Then the "New Order" enveloped that smoldering citadel.
You crawled out of cellars and sewers and rubble,

From behind barricades and antitank traps,
And bomb-crater gaps,
Close to collapse,
Bloody and dirty and dazed,
Half-crazed
With hunger and thirst and the Stukas and the smell.
You were given three days, more or less,
To clean up the mess—
The fifty thousand dead,
The piles of wounded, the blood,
The heaps of bloated horses,
The dust and desolation underfoot,
The horror overhead—
Then the triumphant forces,
The goose-stepping boot,
The twenty-four hours of license to loot,
The newsreel cameras, the trucks loaded with baited bread,
The bands playing waltzes—tootle—toot—toot.

For Der Führer loves his music; he loves it loud and long,
His ears may cringe and quiver, but his stomach is quite
        strong:
So they blasted Chopin's statue
To the bleat of German brass,
And shipped the melted metal to the Berchtesgaden ass.
(One more insult leveled at you;
Write it down—and let it pass.)

26

Write down the whole horrible inventory
Of murder and massacre and plunder:
Record the appalling story
In all its minutiae, howsoever gory—
The sacking of each home, each laboratory,
Each library, church, convent, museum—the ripping asunder
Of beds, the burning of books, the carts groaning under
Their daily hauls,
The people falling flat on their faces
From bullets or hunger, in all kinds of places,
The blood-splattered walls,
The knocking on doors in the night,
The driving like cattle, the faces dead-white,
The vast slaughterhouse from which there is no flight;
Executions en masse
By electric shock or lethal gas,
Or, lined up along self-dug trenches,
And shot in the back of the head,
Or rotting in labor camps, or dropping dead
In the streets with their incredible stenches;
The women parceled out as wenches
For the pleasure of privates and officers—precise blueprint
        of extermination
Of the Pole by every vicious device of annihilation.

Hate, Poles, hate!
Young and old,
Early and late,

Warm your bones against the cold,
Eat and drink from this implacable plate!
Oh, hold
Hate like a lump of ice in your souls!
Let it burn holes
In your heart of hearts, O Poles!

You are not forgotten, Polish people:
The hour of liberation
For your nation
Will soon ring out from every steeple
Of your heroic land.
Through the thick curtain of steel and starvation and terror
          and silence we hear you.
Listen; we are creeping near you—
By Queen Jadwiga's love, by King Jagiello's lance,
What proud Paderewski dreamed, what brave Pilsudski
          planned—
The dawn of your deliverance
Flames at hand!

LETTER TO AN ENGLISH FRIEND

The flame, the carnage, and the battle lust
Are paper darts that peck at walls of stone:
For there are habits in man's marrow bone
Defiant of the bomb, the bayonet thrust:
The cannon's mouth grows brave with birds and rust,
The tank provides a moth his private throne,
The morning stars outsing the clarion,
The moon revisits our victorious dust.

Let us remember rivers and long nights,
And horses with slow bells in each broad hoof,
Hot coffee and cold mornings and quick lights,
And warm rains splashing on a summer roof;
Let us remember, though wars rage between,
The bronze flies roaring softly in the screen.

LETTER TO THE UNCONQUERABLE DUTCH

Trapped between the Devil
And the deep blue sea,
You were laid level
With your long neutrality.
What is good faith good for?
Everything honor and decency stood for:
This is what you spill your blood for:
This is war.
The Devil is cunning; the blue sea is deep.
So you slept, warm in your woolly innocence, and free;
So you slumbered,
Not dreaming your days of liberty were numbered.
Ah, sleep no more, Holland, sleep no more;
The Gauleiter of Darkness, the Overlord of Evil,
Hitler hath murdered sleep.

On they come,
The bringers of the New Millennium
Of hunger, cold, disease, and death to Christendom.
Double, double, toil and trouble,
Rotterdam's a heap of rubble,
And the thirty thousand slain
On that sunny afternoon
Will not bother much again—
At least, not soon.
As for Rembrandt, well, he painted;

Heyermans, he wrote some plays;
Vondel sang a song or two;
Tromp, de Ruyter fought a few,
And de Groot's not hard to praise;
And Spinoza—pfah, a Jew!
All you Dutch are soft and tainted:
These are different times and ways.

So the Nazi Lorelei
Sang the little lamb to bed,
Heard his pretty prayers, and said
With a sigh:
"Though I hate to see you dead
(No one suffers more than I)
Clearly you must die."

Your gallant little water-cradled land
Created by your head and heart and hand,
The labor and the love of people driven
Under a furious dream to build a haven
That should forever stand
A green and pleasant sanctuary
For the oppressed,
Wherein the heavy-laden and the weary
Might come to rest
(Nay, even the Nazi wolf, in innocent lamb's wool dressed,
Found comfort at your breast)—
Yet this brave guileless home

31

Of the free spirit long had been a busy honeycomb
For Hunnish "tourists" and their contemptible underlings
Who ate your bread and planned
This deviltry "on demand,"
And for a medal by the foul fiend blest
And blood-soaked guilder jingling in the vest
Betrayed the thousand fiercely loved familiar things
That used to mean a country where all men walked like kings.

How merrily did the Master Race measure
Along the cloudless heaven at their leisure
The massacre of Rotterdam,
Opening their bomb-bays oh so slowly,
Tasting the fine deliberate pleasure
Like something holy;
As one might sow an acre freshly plowed,
So they sowed flame and death into the crowd.
(It was a perfect afternoon for such:
The sky clear, not a cloud.
As for these stubborn stupid Dutch,
You cannot teach them much;
They're altogether too proud
To be allowed.)

The storybooks would call you "quaint":
We used to hear
Of windmills, cheese and beer,
And thrift and wooden shoes and solid cheer,

Of pious tolerance and proud restraint
And truth without a taint,
And long-bowled pipes and faces fresh as paint,
And tulips that appear
With April's punctual chanticleer.
That Holland died this year.
That kingdom by the sea
Was murdered in cold blood and treachery.
A century
Of peace in five spring days
Perished among the tulips in full blaze,
Sprawled dead among the hyacinths whose sweet smell
Heralded this last loveliest of Mays
And hell
As well.
There are offenses so foul,
So rank
In the black chronicle of crime
They give the soul
So huge a wrench
As leaves an everlasting stench
In the nostrils of time:
So the Rotterdam horror stank.
Even the murky aboriginal demon
At ambush in the breast of slave and freeman
Shrinks from it,
And conscience itself recoils and sickens in one enormous
            vomit.

Before their honest and bewildered eyes,
Men dropping from the skies
In Dutch disguise—
(Behold, the apostles of the new heroic morality
Of treachery
And lechery
And lies.)
"We do not come as enemies,"
They blandly said,
And put a bullet through the farmer's head
And left him dead
In his own tulip bed;
The cattle graze
In the green meadows.
They gaze
At the ballooning shadows
That sway and fall and rise and run together
And fill this quiet weather
At a breath
With shots, confusion, terror, blood, and death.

Policemen, firemen, letter carriers, nuns
Bristling suddenly with hand grenades and guns.
(That amiable next-door neighbor,
The pastry cook's continually smiling lodger
Whose lip curled livid with an old slash of the saber—
Funny codger—
The bicycle-shop-keeper so droll and solemn,

Whose pockets were always bulging with odds and ends—
All these good neighbors, good friends:
The Fifth Column!)

Five days and nights of tumult lewd and vague
And monstrous like some vile nightmarish mist
Swarmed over the Hague;
The plague
Enveloped the Moerdijk Bridge as with a slippery fist.
Forget nothing; warm your hearts with the heroic list:
Remember Waalhaven and the sailors fallen
With that good gallant vessel the *Van Galen*.
Remember, through proud tears,
The battle of Kornwerderzand;
The brave little band
Of Grenadiers
Storming the airdromes, again and again, re-forming
Their shattered lines for still another storming.
Remember, all the days of your years,
That when the world stood tottering and shaken
The dyke of the Zuider Zee was never taken.
Remember the night
Of Venlo and the dynamite. . . .
Remember . . . forget nothing . . . fight . . . fight . . . fight . . .

THE RISING TIDE

The sea is hushed; that vast estate
Stands brimming with the moon;
The new tide gathers in a spate,
The sands commence to sibilate,
The great surf rises soon.

The great surf gathers with the sound
Of people rending chains apart;
Not in one place but all around
Through eyes and ears and nostrils pound
The angers of the heart.

The angers of the heart awake
The sleepers muttering in their sleep;
The tides of terror brim and break,
The winds and whirlwinds rise and rake
The world from deep to deep.

The twisted lump, the spattered wall,
The ax, the rope, the rack, the rifle,
The hearts that burst, the heads that fall—
This is rebellion's clarion call
No tyranny can stifle.

There is no time now to forget,
There is no time now to remember;
The stains are still too warm, too wet,
We keep the count, we mark the debt,
We ring in red the number.

We write in blood from ground and gate,
From bleeding mouth, from gaping brow
We write the record of our hate,
We write the promise of their fate,
We write it here and now.

It grows, a terrible living tide
Of hate and hope and hot despair:
The patriot's and assassin's pride,
The wrath of the tyrannicide
Flame in the fetid air.

The sea is hushed; that vast estate
Stands brimming with the moon;
The new tide gathers in a spate,
The sands commence to sibilate,
The great surf rises soon.

LETTER TO THE UNCONQUERABLE BELGIANS

"Of all
The peoples which inhabit Gaul,"
Caesar said,
"The Belgians are
The most courageous by far,
Being continually at war
With the barbarians beyond the Rhine. . . ."
By the long centuries of your deathless dead,
O, shine
Forever forth, immortal star
Of Belgium, now as then,
To Belgian patriots—and to all men!

It is not finished;
It has happened before;
You have heard the Teuton roar
Too many times with fury undiminished,
Not to know
The ancient fiend and the eternal foe;
Nevertheless, you will more
Than even the score;
Though meanwhile you must wait,
Your hearts stretched to the bursting point with hate,
Your children dying,
Or, by God's mercy, dead
(At least, that stops their crying),

Because the Beast denies them bread—
(Alas, for the unborn! Alas, for the disinherited!)
Your young men and women herded into cars like cattle
To the accompaniment of the machine guns' rattle,
Driven at the point of bayonet and saber
To slave labor:
Where, and in what corner of Nazi hell,
Who can tell;
Unless that unspeakable traitor,
That pipsqueak Quisling and collaborator,
Léon Degrelle,
Knows; unless he knows
The beatings, the blows,
The rapes,
The "fixed" and fatal escapes,
The deliberate provocations and "incidents,"
The horrors of the concentration camp,
Impromptu fiendishness the Nazi mind invents,
The casual massacres of innocents—
Men, women, children, old and young,
Mowed down some drizzling dawn in a gray yard
By a firing squad as cold and hard
And damp,
And left there for the flies like so much dung.

Hunger has made you weak,
But still you speak
With a voice as strong

As a trumpet's tongue,
In *La Libre Belgique*.
The Nazi gnaws his fingernails;
The Gestapo hunts here and there
And everywhere
To find you—and fails;
Once in a while
A boy is tortured, a weakling is bought,
A hero is caught:
Then a smile
Creases the Commandant's mouth and eyes,
And one more patriot stands up against a wall and dies. . . .
Still the big heart of Belgium beats underground
(Two hundred secret newspapers make a magnificent sound),
Hums like hushed hard thunder
Deep down under,
Throbs softly and insistently all around,
And is never found;
The unconquerable Belgian soul
Is carried from hand to hand
Like a hot coal;
It is only a spark
Cupped dangerously in the dark.
And yet this irrepressible subterranean antic
Has driven, and will drive, the Nazis frantic:
Some twenty-five years since or so
It told the Boche in Belgium where to go;
Now, in a fierce rebirth,

It blazes with sardonic mirth
To all the hunted men in all the earth:
La Libre Belgique! La Libre Belgique!
Punctually, week by week,
The scornful headline
Meets the deadline;
Nor can
The whole Gestapo catch or conquer Peter Pan,
Nor ever bring to heel
The Fleming spirit's mercury and steel.

When a just vengeance rolls the drum,
Truth's fixed inflexible finger will determine
The valiant from the vermin
In Belgium's massive martyrdom:
Who stood up to the German,
Who found it safer to succumb;
The agent in the ditch,
With his cropped ugly head
Bashed to an uglier red,
Will point out which is which;
The bridge bombed, train derailed,
The factory that failed,
The ship that never sailed—
These, when the lengthening list
Of saboteur and incendiarist
Is at the last unveiled—
These battles will be hallowed, these heroes will be hailed.

And there are others, many, many others:
Anonymous nun and nameless priest,
Whose martyrdom has never ceased;
The little sisters and heroic brothers
Of the Church,
Whom the Nazi Devil of the twisted foot
Seeks vainly to uproot,
To besmirch:
Calm shepherds of the flock,
They strive against the Beast,
They stand against the Antichrist,
A refuge and a rock.

There is an old cathedral in Ghent,
Saint Bavon is the name,
Where visitors from every country came
And went
To see *The Adoration of the Lamb*
By Jan van Eyck that hung upon the wall
Of a chapel dusty and dark and small.

For five hundred years or so
It had been hanging in that humble chapel,
Making the dingy little room glow;
For five hundred years,
For generations,
Pilgrimages of people,
Of all faiths and nations,

Had climbed those cathedral stairs
To gaze through sudden tears
At this miracle of innumerable adorations;
To stand hushed before the soul, the heart,
The dreams and aspirations
Of the Flemish race:
All the science, poetry, religion, art
Distilled in the pure imperishable glory
Of a face;
The strength and hope of a time, a place,
A people telling their story.

And now this luminous mirror
Of an ancient and heroic people's spirit
Adorns, to the whole world's horror,
The house
Of Meinherr Göring and his ponderous spouse.
(How shall the conscience of humanity bear it?)
For this foul murderer of the Luftwaffe, this
Boisterous elephant adores
Paintings and statues and tapestries by the scores
(All nobly kidnaped, of course);
And now the Ghent cathedral altarpiece,
His latest "guest,"
Perhaps his loveliest,
Inflames our Nordic Falstaff's breast!

Ah well, let him enjoy his feast—
Beauty and the Beast:
It happened once before
In the last war—
The Germans looted the same loveliness, the same.
Who knows but it may tame
The monster a little; at all events
The glory that was Ghent's
Will one day be restored
In God's good hour, with Belgium's faith and fame,
To flame
In all its unpolluted lineaments
Before the Lord.

THESE EVENINGS

These evenings when the stars increase
To crowd the calyx moon with petals,
Upon the heart unearthly peace
Like some rich pollen settles.

Though heart and stars must both observe
The blood-flushed Four, the blood-flecked Horses,
And know that nothing now can swerve
Those couriers from their courses.

Not the slow glory of this hour,
The gleam of night, the overflowing
Of the moon's pale enormous flower
Can stop the heart from knowing.

LETTER TO THE UNCONQUERABLE GREEKS

I write this letter to you on my knees
In the night,
O people of a thousand Thermopylaes,
And every word I write,
If it be worthy somehow in your sight—
Sons of Solon, daughters of Pericles—
Will blaze with light.

Regard this letter
As token payment long since overdue
From your eternal debtor—
An echo burning through
The silence and the death piled thick on you
By fire and sword, by famine and by fetter—
An echo of the trumpet Plato blew
Across another darkness that men knew.

Not by an honorable foe
In equal combat, blow for blow,
Under a decent sky,
Beneath the impartial sun,
Were you undone
And left to die.
Ah no!
But by each slippery ruse
Buzzard and jackal use;

Stalked by that obscene pack
In stealthy and abominable attack,
Struck down at last when faint with hunger,
You could no longer
Stand and strike back.

And when you fell, you fell like some great star,
Not broken by defeat or pale surrender,
But falling in dreadful splendor,
Forever falling and falling.
And earth and heaven and the towers of time both near
            and far
Were shaken with the shouts of terror calling,
And the blood-red wheels of war,
Bright and brawling,
Across the firmament streaked a livid scar.

So you went down, yet, in your dying, cast
A shadow across the craters of the moon as vast,
As bright,
As the Archangel's trumpet blast
Of light,
A shadow upon the hearts of men as well,
To stretch our souls from heaven down to hell!

This we declare:
By all men in extremity everywhere,
By earth and water, by fire and air,

We solemnly swear:
Homer is not dead;
The loins that bred
Ulysses will again
Beget such men
(The spirit of Bozzaris, of Byron,
The Mavrocordatos breed
Of iron.)
This is our creed:
The sun
That sees
Fascist and Hun
Cleansed from the land
Of Demosthenes
Will once more in amazement stare upon
The Parthenon!

This, then, is all;
I have said everything;
The wormwood, the gall,
The courage, the suffering;
Nothing can be
As big as agony,
And agony is king, and can speak
Only in Greek.

And the Greek
Continues to speak

With dagger and bomb
And bullet, at home;
With his hero dead
Staining the Libyan sands a richer red;
With his sailor brave
In his eternally wandering grave;
With his pilot, proud and impetuous,
The modern Icarus,
Adding bright plumes of power and grace
To the wings of Samothrace!

When the battle is done,
When the victory is won,
May the spirit and glory
Of each Greek daughter and son
Find the singer of their dark immortal story
In some new Xenophon,
And in the pride and tears of liberated Greece
Her heroes find forever green their laurels and their peace.

ELEGY IN AUTUMN
(For a Friend Fallen in Battle)

I heard the geese go over in the night
With harsh and punctual horns, black wedge on wedge,
Launching the spearheads of their autumn flight,
Fulfilling some fierce migratory pledge.

The prows of Carthage and the long-oared Norse,
Under diverse stars and in seas remote,
Stared up at that same cry, high-pitched and hoarse,
And felt the same strange tightening of the throat.

Here on a hilltop in my homeland waken
Those cold old echoes in a throaty tangle,
And something heavier than the heart is shaken,
And great forgotten knots of memory strangle.

I heard the geese go over and go over,
I heard the wild geese going, spear on spear,
I heard them crying to a fellow rover
Who last fall stood and heard them crying here.

LETTER TO THE UNCONQUERABLE LUXEMBOURGERS

You are so small, O Luxembourg, so small,
But proud:
A land
No bigger than a cloud
Like a man's hand,
Or the shadow of a man on a wall;
Nevertheless, when the horn of hate,
The tocsin of your fate
Rang loud,
The blunt barbarian at the gate
Found you erect, contemptuous, uncowed.

You were an old and quiet place,
An ancient and a courteous race
Of culture, courage, godliness, and grace;
The traveler drank your golden wine;
He saw green fields with kine
Deep in the fragrant grasses or knee-deep
In some sweet stream
Like figures in a landscape in a dream;
He saw an occasional flock
Of sheep
Pink-gilt or silver-dusty in the sun,
The shepherd sound asleep
Against a shadowy rock . . .
(Alas, these four long years now overrun

By the recurrent tidal Hun!)
And yet this peaceful duchy, this most pleasant realm
Wave after wave of Vandals overwhelm,
Leaving in their tempestuous wake
Horror, destruction, carnage, and blood to shake
The spirit they will never break.

These are the little people—and the list
Is long—
Who have no champion elsewhere, and no song,
Save that their souls are strong
Beneath the weight of wrong;
Beneath a throng
Of iron edicts they resist,
By silent hate, revenge and sudden death,
By sabotage of the bold arsonist,
With their last drop of blood, with their last breath,
The brutal omnipresent Fist.

Nothing the Nazis do, or shall have done,
Can interrupt the slow invincible tale
Of liberation
For you, proud little nation;
It cannot fail:
No fury, on however vast a scale,
Can frighten or prevail,
Or by a single hour postpone
The day of wrath; not by an hour, not one,
Delay their setting, and your rising, sun.

TARGET FOR TONIGHT

Serenely through a sea of stars
The moon of autumn rides,
Blind to our wounds, deaf to our wars,
But tyrant of our tides.

From her indifferent wrist depends
A silver punctual chain
That harnesses to restless ends
The rhythms of the rain.

Upon unholy calendars
Men mark their blood-drenched Ides. . . .
Serenely through a sea of stars
The moon of autumn rides.

LETTER TO THE UNCONQUERABLE YUGOSLAVS

Butchery cannot curb
The lionhearted Serb;
The man hunt, torture, bribe,
The whole immense machine,
Fantastic and obscene,
No language can describe—
Find Croat and Slovene
One fierce unconquerable tribe.

Throughout the long flame-dark five hundred years
Of blood and battle and terror and tears:
From Murad the Turk,
From the red spiked axles of the charioteers,
From the turbans and the terraced spears,
From the horsehair plumes, the dagger, the dirk,
From the arrows that drank deep of the infidel's throat,
The wolf's howl, the hawk's note,
The silence and assurance of the goat,
The desperate skills and ardors learned by rote;
Through oceans of time and agony,
Through the salt-sweet fertility
Of death in the valleys of the deathless land
Of the South Slav; by the crags that stand
Under the night's eternal eye,
Horns locked in black embrace against the Balkan sky;
By freedom's blaze and breath, passion and pride,

Through savage centuries the Yugoslav defied
His enemies—and died.

And still he lives, chainless in chains, and free,
This fierce unfettered child of the Chetniki;
Once more he beats the guerrilla drums
Of his fathers;
His heart like thunder gathers,
His heart's blood hums:
Sing, Chetnik, sing
Till your wild mountains ring!
From Balkan darkness and from Balkan sorrow
Let exultation and defiance borrow
New hope, new faith, fresh courage for the morrow;
Lift up your hearts in song until
The Butcher's blood turns chill
(The blood your naked knives know how to spill):
"Without warning, without warning, as the lightning crackles,
Swoop, guerrillas, swoop, guerrillas, on the Hitler jackals!
Bombs are bursting now; Germans stagger;
Crimson gleams the tongue of every Chetnik dagger!" . . .

His courage is his countrymen's;
His mountains attend him:
The secret glens,
The goat-guarded peaks,
The gorges, the caves and dens—
All know him, all defend him;

And when the man hunt harries
And hems his hiding place,
He eats wolves, grass, roots, berries,
And laughs into his foeman's face,
And leaves no trace. . . .
Nay, even when his great wounds gape and bleed
And grievously spend him,
When his hot strength goes out of him and his need
Is sorest,
His old mother, the forest,
Folds him in her bosom; leaf speaks
To leaf; the falcons befriend him,
The running rivers mend him. . . .

What if the school, the spire,
The village, the tall city
Are blotted out entire,
Are leveled without pity—
Kragujevac, Belgrade:
Burnt corpses on parade;
Necks cocked at grotesque angle,
The tortured martyrs dangle,
The dead men dance askew
Full in the public view—
Forever shall they smolder
In hearts whose hate leaps higher
Than any mountain's shoulder,
Than any wall of fire.

Whisper their name in the mountains;
The mountains will shout it back
To the mournful valleys and fields and fountains,
To the proud women in black:
To the daughters of the nine sons of Yug Bogdan
Whose lavish manhood hallowed Kossovo's Plain,
To their daughters' daughters' daughters who see falling
(Hear the hawks and mountains calling . . . calling . . .)
Over and over and over again
The same red stain,
The same holy and heroic rain. . . .

Soon, gallant Yugoslavs, oh soon
Your sons and daughters will hold hands again and dance
The *kolo* under the brilliant Balkan moon:
Their lustrous eyes will glance,
Their goatskin moccasins weave the ancient tune
Of gypsy flute and bagpipe; their long hair
Glistening like black light
By the moon-flecked fountains of the public square
In the peaceful Balkan night.

DUNKERQUE ANNIVERSARY

When the beast from the dark primordial slime
Bellowed his hunger for blood and bone,
When the Czech stood stalwart and sublime
Against the tusks of the mastodon,
When the Pole was gored for the hundredth time,
When the Fleming's furious fate was known,
When the Dutch and the French blazed blood and grime—
England elected to fight alone.

For nine incredible nights and days,
Beneath the pounding of bomb and gun,
Beneath the infernal heat and haze,
Beneath the pitiless blood-drenched sun,
On the Norman beach's glare and glaze
The weaponless Tommy faced the Hun,
And while we could only gasp and gaze
England elected to fight alone.

When the Stukas droned their savagery,
And it seemed no strength could stop that drone,
A small and a gallant company
Hurled that hellish armada down,
Wrought an eagle-defended Thermopylae,
Laughing at death from a treacherous throne:
Pillared in flame between sky and sea,
England elected to fight alone.

From Beowulf, Alfred and Harold on,
From Arthur and Armstrong and Robin Hood,
This is the breed of Bellerophon,
This is the Lion's fearless brood,
This is the Balaclava blood,
This is the creed of the Camperdown:
When all but the soul is quite subdued,
England elects to fight alone.

Now that we face the foe as one,
The foul implacable fiend, none other,
Eternally cunning, the ruthless Hun,
Now that we stand as brother with brother,
Now that the enemy is known,
Now that we rally round our Mother,
Until the beast in his own blood smother,
England no longer fights alone.

ABOUT THE AUTHOR

JOSEPH AUSLANDER, author, editor, educator, lecturer, and Philadelphian, was educated at Harvard and the Sorbonne. He has published several volumes of verse, edited anthologies, and won various prizes. Since 1937 consultant in poetry for the Library of Congress, he also roves around the country gathering in important manuscripts and other literary treasures for the Library. He is married to Audrey Wurdemann, Pulitzer Prize winner for poetry in 1937, and has one child, a daughter.

A Representative Selection of
Simon and Schuster Publications

THE BIBLE DESIGNED TO BE READ AS LIVING LITERATURE
edited by ERNEST SUTHERLAND BATES

A TREASURY OF ART MASTERPIECES: FROM THE RENAISSANCE
TO THE PRESENT DAY *edited by* THOMAS CRAVEN

A TREASURY OF GILBERT AND SULLIVAN *edited by* DEEMS TAYLOR,
illustrated by LUCILLE CORCOS

A TREASURY OF THE THEATRE: AN ANTHOLOGY OF GREAT PLAYS
FROM AESCHYLUS TO EUGENE O'NEILL *edited by*
BURNS MANTLE *and* JOHN GASSNER

MEN OF ART *and* MODERN ART *edited by* THOMAS CRAVEN

VAN LOON'S GEOGRAPHY *and* THE ARTS *by* HENDRIK WILLEM VAN LOON

THE EVOLUTION OF PHYSICS *by* ALBERT EINSTEIN *and* LEOPOLD INFELD

A TREASURY OF THE WORLD'S GREAT LETTERS
edited by M. LINCOLN SCHUSTER

A SECOND TREASURY OF THE WORLD'S GREAT LETTERS *edited by*
WALLACE BROCKWAY *and* BART KEITH WINER

THE ART OF THINKING *by* ABBÉ ERNEST DIMNET

SHORT STORIES FROM THE NEW YORKER

THIRTY-TWO SONATAS OF LUDWIG VAN BEETHOVEN
edited by ARTUR SCHNABEL

THE STORY OF PHILOSOPHY *and* THE STORY OF CIVILIZATION
by WILL DURANT

THE VICTOR BOOK OF THE SYMPHONY *by* CHARLES O'CONNELL

THE VICTOR BOOK OF THE OPERA

LIVING PHILOSOPHIES: A SYMPOSIUM *by* ALBERT EINSTEIN,
H. G. WELLS, *et al.*

I BELIEVE: THE PERSONAL PHILOSOPHIES OF CERTAIN EMINENT
MEN AND WOMEN OF OUR TIME, *edited with an*
introduction by CLIFTON FADIMAN

READING I'VE LIKED *edited by* CLIFTON FADIMAN

MISSION TO MOSCOW *by* AMBASSADOR JOSEPH E. DAVIES

The Inner Sanctum edition of WAR AND PEACE

VICTORY THROUGH AIR POWER *by* MAJOR ALEXANDER P. DE SEVERSKY